Child's Guide to the Holy Days

Immaculate Conception

Christmas

Mary, Mother of God

Ascension of the Lord

The Assumption

All Saints' Day

KATHY DELLATORRE O'KEEFE

ILLUSTRATIONS BY ANNE CATHARINE BLAKE

Paulist Press
New York/Mahwah, N.J.

This book is dedicated to two special mothers—
Mary, the mother of Jesus,
and in memory of my own mother, Virginia DellaTorre—
for their loving guidance through the years!
KDTO

For my little granddaughter,
Aurora Sage
ACB

Caseside design by Sharyn Banks
Caseside illustration by Anne Catharine Blake

Text Copyright © 2007 by Kathy DellaTorre O'Keefe
Illustrations Copyright © 2007 by Anne Catharine Blake

Library of Congress Cataloging-in-Publication Data

O'Keefe, Kathy DellaTorre.
    Child's guide to the holy days / Kathy DellaTorre O'Keefe; illustrations by Anne Catharine Blake.
    p. cm.
    ISBN-13: 978-0-8091-6731-9 (alk. paper)
    1. Fasts and feasts—Catholic Church—Juvenile literature. I. Blake, Anne Catharine. II. Title.
    BV30.045 2007
    263'.9—dc22

                                                                    2006015108

Published by Paulist Press
997 Macarthur Boulevard
Mahwah, New Jersey 07430

www.paulistpress.com

Printed and bound in Mexico

Welcome! My name is Maggie.

I'm writing a school report on the **Holy Days of Obligation.** In my report, I'm pretending to travel back in time over two thousand years. I want to show what happened back then that makes each of these days holy.

I'm so glad you're coming with me. Along the way we'll discover what a holy day of obligation is and why we celebrate each one.

First, what's an obligation? An *obligation* is a *duty*, something we *should* do. Our duty on holy days is to go to Mass. Sometimes the holy day is celebrated during regular Sunday Mass, sometimes during the week, and there is a special Mass. Whether the Mass is on Sunday or another day depends on what country you live in and on your diocese.

A *diocese* is a group of churches under one bishop. Different dioceses have slightly different rules, the way families have slightly different rules. For example, one family opens presents on Christmas Eve, another on Christmas morning, and yet another when relatives arrive the day after Christmas. They are all still celebrating! No matter when a holy day is celebrated, it brings us together to share God's love as one big family in the Church.

At Mass we listen to readings from the Bible. The readings tell us about God and what happened many, many years ago in faraway places. We remember the good people who brought God's word to us. And each year we learn more about the life of Jesus as we celebrate the holy days.

Can you name any holy days right now? In the United States, we celebrate six of them.

Let's begin our adventure at a time when there was no Christmas or Easter. Mary, Jesus' mother, wasn't even born yet.

Look close by the fire. The woman stirring something in the large pot is St. Anne. She's going to have a baby, and that baby will grow up to be Mary.

From the very beginning of Mary's life or her *conception*—which means even while she was still inside her mother's body—Mary was free from original sin. Original sin is the sin of Adam and Eve. The result of that sin is passed on to everyone who has ever lived, except for Mary and, of course, Jesus.

There is a special holy day to honor this event in Mary's life. We call this holy day the feast of the **Immaculate Conception**. *Immaculate* means clean and pure. We go to Mass for the Immaculate Conception on either December 8 or the closest Sunday.

The next stop is my favorite. We're going to a little town called Bethlehem.

See the crowd of people. Can you find Mary riding on the donkey? Her husband Joseph is walking beside her.

They're looking for a place to sleep. There is no room anywhere. They decide to rest in a stable filled with animals and hay. Can you name the animals you see with Mary and Joseph?

During the night something wonderful happens! A baby boy is born to Mary. His name is Jesus, and he is our Savior.

Do you know what holy day this is?
Yes, it's **Christmas**! And we always celebrate Christmas on December 25.

To thank Mary for bringing Jesus into the world, the Church chose another special day. Let's find out about it.

See the beautiful girl praying beneath the window. That's Mary praying to God.

Before Mary became the mother of Jesus, when she was still just a girl, God sent the angel Gabriel to ask her if she was willing to do this. And she said, "Yes!"

God chose her from all the women who ever lived. To thank Mary for saying "Yes" to God, the Church honors her with the holy day called **Mary, Mother of God**. Sometimes it is also called the **Solemnity of Mary**. *Solemnity* means highest honor. That's the best! We go to Mass for Mary, Mother of God on January 1 or the closest Sunday.

Let's keep exploring!

Did you know that after Jesus died and was raised from the dead, he came back to earth for forty days? During that time he visited his friends, including the apostles.

Let's go inside the room. Everyone looks surprised and happy to see Jesus. Can you count how many of his friends are standing beside him?

By coming back to earth, Jesus showed the entire world he truly is the risen Christ. This helps us to believe that God loves us very much.

At the end of the forty days, Jesus returned to heaven to be with his Father. The Church calls this holy day the **Ascension of the Lord**. To *ascend* means to move or rise up. See in the picture how Jesus' hands are lifted up toward heaven to greet his Father.

We celebrate the Ascension of the Lord around forty days after Easter. The exact date changes every year, depending on when Easter is. In some dioceses the Mass for it is celebrated on a Thursday, in some on a Sunday.

Our journey now takes us to a time just after Mary's life has ended. Right after she died, something extraordinary happened.

Mary was lifted up to heaven with both her soul *and* her body.

The Church calls this holy day the feast of Mary's **Assumption**. *Assumed* means that Mary was taken up body and soul into the glory of heaven. We can imagine Jesus welcoming Mary with a big hug! Some dioceses go to Mass for the Assumption on August 15, some on the closest Sunday.

Our next holy day gives us a peek at a great place—heaven! I wonder who we might find there?

Look, I can see my grandma and grandpa holding hands with each other. Can you find my Aunt Lucy? She's waving at me.

Do you see St. Anne, Mary's mother? Can you find St. Joseph? And there's St. Francis of Assisi in the brown robe.

Did you know that *you* could be a saint one day, too? You need to be a very good person, to do what's right, and to love God! Then the Church will celebrate a holy day in *your* honor too! It's called **All Saints' Day.** Some dioceses go to Mass for it on November 1, others on the nearest Sunday.

On this day we remember *everyone* now in heaven with God. No matter how long they've been there or who they are, everyone in heaven is a *saint*. There are some saints that everyone knows about—and we put the word *Saint* before their name, like St. Francis or St. Thérèse or St. Joseph. There are also many good people in heaven that no one knows about, maybe only their family and friends. And if you're in heaven, you're a saint! So this day is for everyone.

Now that our journey is about to end, I have a surprise for you!
Did you know that every Sunday is also a holy day?

There is a Sunday called **Easter Sunday** that is truly awesome! The third day after Jesus died, some friends came to his tomb to place oils on his body. But when they arrived at the place he was buried, he was gone! See the lady carrying the oils? She and her friend look sad and worried because Jesus is not in the tomb.

They forgot his promise to rise on the third day to open the gates of heaven to everyone!

We remember Easter Sunday now by going to Mass *every* Sunday. After we go to Mass, God also wants us to do something else. He wants us to stop work, to relax, and to spend time with our family and friends. He wants us to enjoy the wonderful life he has given us!

Will you accept God's invitation to come to Mass and celebrate the Holy Days of Obligation with him?